CH00406806

Haiku and Senryu

A book for Beginners
by a Beginner

Haiku and Senryu

A book for Beginners
by a Beginner

Brian Jarvis

Haiku and Senryu

A Book for Beginners by a Beginner

Paperback: ISBN 978-1-3999-5251-4

Copyright © 2023 Brian Jarvis

All rights reserved.

Published by Brian Jarvis Publications

ACKNOWLEDGEMENTS

Some of the images reproduced in this book have been designed using assets from **www.Freepik.com** for which we are grateful. These include the photograph on the front cover and title page, and some of the small images at the top of the poetry pages.

The Author and Publisher also acknowledge a number of original photographs, reproduced on single pages, taken by **Graham and Sue Wade** during a recent visit to Japan.

Preface

English original verses by the author

A few words of further explanation from the author:

"The following Verses on this page, and what you encounter in this book, are the author's original work — in English. They follow and honour Japanese 'short-form' Haiku and Senryu poetry. Ancient, they, in translation for a century or more, have 'opened up' in the West, and fostered mass appreciation of their brevity, pithiness, insights and beauty."

The author adds the following two verses here:

Philosophy's words –
concepts known, practice needed:
worthy search for Truth

May all Beginners
perceive that subtle moment
original Verse

Author's wish and hopes
Spring/Summer 2023

About the Author, Brian Jarvis

Now aged 86, the author's published life-story is called *'A minor life of Brian'* – he so much enjoyed the rather indelicate Monty Python film. Modesty says this Book of verse might be seen *in the same minor light* !

A long retired journalist and PR man, he for 50 years has studied and 'tried to live' practical philosophy. He has also written a play on the Quaker martyr Mary Dyer who died in Boston 1660, and several websites on religion and political subjects. However, he says that writing this book has been "The most marvellous and challenging literary finale".

The author thanks his great friend Chris Dell for being Consultant and IT/Computer 'expediter' for this book.

Also many thanks to Riccardo Santini for his expert assistance in creating the cover design in Photoshop.

Brian Jarvis   Chris Dell

Efforts are sole — mine ?
or indeed are WE, all, One:
the richer is clear

Contents

Introduction to ʜaiku and Senʀyu

Honouring Japanese ʜistorical origins but in today's English oʀiginal verses

Hello. Welcome to this Haiku and Senryu 'A ʙook for Beginners by a Beginner' — a book of original short-form verʂe grouped under different headings (needed to break up what wouʆᵈ ᵒtherwise be a cumbersome unvaried offering for you, the reader). Thᵉ ɪʳst two main headings are **Haiku: Nature/Seasons**, and **Everyday/Senᵣyᵤ**. This book is indeed a Work-in-Progress. It is hoped that Beginners aᵗtempting Japanese-style haiku and senryu in the English language will ᵗᵃiɴ from reading and re-working some of the verses – as I will continue to ᵈo!

From first 'taking up' haiku, writing, assessing, judging and improving is the path ahead – besides continuing to consult the works of wise experienced practitioners. Haiku and senryu 'one-deep-breath' stand-alone verses arise from our keen perceptions, encompass intuitions and can present startling insights — they can surprise us with their 'Aha!' gentle surprise OR cause unexpected shock; and modify even enlarge our view of our environment and the world. They can be so enjoyable – fresh air and innocence in the moment as one poet has said; they can counter our ordinary worldly experiences which often lead us into to boredom, even some stale cynicism.

In this Work-in-Progr... re verses are grouped under three
...ther main headings: **P**.../**Psychology**; **Spirit**; and **Potpourri** —
and it is quite und... that many esteemed, experienced,
'traditionalist' and '... practitioners will take exception to such
headings (further au... explanation will be made later).

They, the pra... ...ers, much admired by this author, have had so
much more to s... ...bout haiku and senryu, particularly benefiting us
Beginners. The... ...od counsel has been so helpful and assimilated for
my abbreviat... ...and compacted General comment/Guidelines offering.

One Japanese source says 'earliest modern-era' haiku (arising from
the 17th -18th century but known in much earlier centuries) are not just
'about Nature' but rather the seasonal changes we might 'see' in and
around and about Nature, animals, plants, the oceans, sky, and
(humanity's daily lives – if we were/are 'awake'. Nobody as far as I
know (among our English-language practitioners) has gone so far as to
claim the perfect 'definitions' of haiku and senryu. There is often a
verse which is easily seen as not haiku nor senryu – it is the 'hybrid'. So
what is the 'norm'? Verses should be brief and (intended) simple to
understand, and reflect keen 'perception' and 'intuition' and 'insight' —
arising in a moment, which we may come to understand as Heightened
awareness.

'The Haiku Moment' is timeless, an experience that stands outside
the normal flow of time, in the 'eternal present', is one poetic view.
Other practitioners explain that as such they can well 'open our (inner,
subtle) eyes' often with that sense of surprise, even a real 'sit up
moderate shock', which has been mentioned even maybe add to our
appreciation of wisdom. For in a good verse, 'We suddenly see into the
(BJ: true, eternal) nature of things'.

Now this is most useful, to us 'Beginners': a ᵤ writer/poet provides the information and you the reade.. resonates with his/her images from within your imagination!' sa, favourite English haiku/senryu poet.

I add – NOT imaginings! We work with the objective lodged in the mind – not the subjective; this does need clarification – later.

I would never (totally) disagree with him, my mentor, but I would qualify – in this, my humble/still exploring viewpoint – in they/our Beginners' appreciation, that what any of our five senses bring into mind/intellect 'perception' can be coarse/fine; brief and shallow/not staying; or so clear and deep — with embedded, never-changing value WHICH can be 'recovered' by a quiet still mind (intellect is deep, where the reflective perception is held, good or a passing trace). MIND however, the servant to our haiku, senryu composition and writing — mind is 'brilliant and often undisciplined' – the Will needs to be in charge!. With still posture, let mind fall quiet: you do not 'think' haiku verses' although there is some release in senryu's naughty forages!

I might/should stop now, here. Let you Beginner go into the Verse (which, of course now you have already skipped through: human nature/ego). Let me continue a little, please.

In English-style, our Haiku and senryu are mostly 'serious and often austere' — short-verse, one-deep-breath, stand-alone 'poems'. They feature a (normal) two-part juxtaposition of images. The first two lines are usually clear, giving a hint of story! Then, 'perception' rather hidden before the last third line appears, are brought out in the mind's eye. The reader may well then 'see' aspects of Nature, seasons experienced as did the 'composer/author in the 'sublime' moment. It could result in in meaningful 'present' — or light laughter!

At their best, they connect us with ourselves, with great Nature from flowers' beauty to tsunami's dreadful impact, and the 'apparently' beyond all, the eternal. Please go look explore great practitioners for yourselves.

And the 'apparently beyond all' — the eternal. Please, Beginner, go look for yourselves. Great practitioners' works often reflect all these 'deeper perceptions'.

I offer this my haiku and several senryuu

> So quiet, I sit
> where are you, you loving bird
> not on tree, outside

Senryu arose, a bit later in the 18th - 19th century and they tend to reflect, comment on human foibles and behaviour. Senryu (attempted by the author) will challenge you to develop this, in your possible senryu. In MY verses, these four 5-7-5, are later in this book:

> From open window,
> two large ladies pass, talking:
> compassion's carers

> She admits the truth –
> never really listening:
> giggles a 'sorry'

> She is so frightened –
> sev'ral come to collect her
> door smashed, she sectioned

> Her so golden voice
> promises hidden virtues:
> her perfect mask slips

Senryu can be gentle and not malicious but just observational OR rather wickedly satirical. They are said to 'parody' the more 'holy' traditional Haiku and mostly use the same structure. Both equally, in their way, can observe the mundane and the sublime. Senryu are more relaxed — poking fun endearingly, often at our behaviour, habits — whether reader, practitioner or Beginner. By many they are today considered a part-genre in their own right — just as 'zappai' verses may be (long seen under the cloud of being mere senryu-like 'doggerel').

More on General comment and Rules, and Guidelines come in the next Chapter. However, it is I hope helpful here to clarify several directions. It is conceded that this is still a Work-in-Progress and it is to be understood that there is some repetition found in parts of the book – considered important to help Beginners re-read, consider more, and assimilate deeper. Secondly, many verses are not in a perfect 5-7-5 pattern, some have minor faults — they can be re-worked, with fresh words, as it is hoped Beginners might undertake, enjoy, and see better what the author/composer was attempting to reveal, and so to learn from. It can be invaluable practice.

Two key features, following the above clarification, are mentioned here, regarding the next Chapter: Haiku are usually three lines of up to/as a maximum 17 English-language 'syllables'. But today's expert practitioners often favour anything from 7-14 syllables, some popular as in 12 (as did, it is said, the 'Japanese Masters' often did).

Haiku verses traditionally contain a Season word (kigo) and a cutting word or 'cut marker' called kireji. The kigo indicates a particular seasonal context, which the reader/listener may pick up on; the kireji is a break, a pause in the verse, often simple English punctuation. The question: to punctuate or not to punctuate (two viewpoints here, the latter having the reader ponder the verse's meaning a bit deeper)?

Our punctuation, in our three-line Haiku or senryu, say esteemed more knowledgeable and argue — can be a help or hindrance. Especially to the Beginner. How does punctuation or no punctuation seem to you, Beginner? now you've explored somewhat, after reading books such as this? AND drafted out some haiku and senryu verses ?

You don't have to answer to me, this author. You answer to yourself, or yourSelf. And your readers. You and I may hope – they will see and feel and know — what those embedded 'perceptions' you experienced, and here have attempted to 'reveal' to them in honour of greater personal 'insights' and educational and societal 'inspirations' — which can lead to 'changing things for the better'.

When a bore starts up
so many Words not needed?
WE *see* through and love

Piano plays softly
You hear orchestra too
'Midsomer Rhapsody'

General/Guidelines

A mix of useful advice?

The following is a mix of **General comments**, about haiku and senryu, and also more **specific Guidelines**. The aim is to help us Beginners 'stay on the right track' in 'versifying' in the western/English language style. As I have willingly, enthusiastically. Beginners becoming attracted to ancient Japanese haiku and senryu, enough to want to compose and write their own original verses, in English, are invited to go seek again and again the more expert published viewpoints on Guidelines by established practitioners.

In what follows there will be **some repetition and re-interpretation** – as wise counsel bears frequent re-stating, re-reading, re-hearing for Beginners. Though in 'the West' since 1920's onwards, what exactly is the 'pure' definition of 'haiku' and 'senryu' is still debated; the basics, principles, what constitutes 'good' verse, are fairly well accepted today.

These lightly held 'rules' help give haiku and senryu such splendid differences from traditional 'poetry'. For these verses ARE poetry. And their often 'zen-like' impact can awake the reader – with surprise, amazement, even awe, OR help you smile in gentle agreement with the writer/author.

The advice from 'the true practitioners' is easily researched. Especially their (abundant) Guidelines, for they are so generous in sharing their understandings. Go search ! Go find! Go assimilate and practise ! Don't worry about their over-rich 'insights' – you'll come through it with better understanding !

Too much 'information' and 'advice'? 'It can impede the haiku poetic impulse', believes one practitioner. Maybe so. Working 5-7-5 verses asks much of us. Including through experience, clear views of 'our inner make-up'. What do – in versifying – we really understand about the inner subtle roles of our individual unique Senses, Perception, Intellect, Mind and words, in the (miraculous too strong a word?) emergence of such startling (OR 'ordinary' !) verses.

Forgive me, I've often pondered: if Shakespeare had come across ancient Japanese haiku; would we, the world not just 'England', have gained, or lost? His challenging sonnets might have dwelt in dusty corners.

The Beginners' challenge is found in: reading the recommended 'rules' and 'best composition' and disciplined use in 'recovering' the gift of 'the true deep and secure perception' brought through the senses, when sharp in the present, reflective as we 'work' on assimilation, understanding and practice,

Repetition has its value. We humans amazingly, see but do not see, hear but do not hear, don't recognise to taste a 'subtle' moment. Mind, our great servant, takes attention elsewhere. We experience the 'grey ghost' of a passing worthy moment. I, awake, once saw a beautiful yellow rose, growing, alone, out of a hedge. What joy !

Their zen-like impact
awakens readers' surprise:
smile at *your* insight !

They are a reflection of ourSel~
poet's view. They are a flash of 'the ~ as 'silent Witness', is
academic psychologist, in the UK, explain~ 'the Moment NOW'. .
'Life consists of **millions of moments**. S~ ago, that for each of us,
moments', he said 'Mindfulness is *to be*' belie~, in terms of 'Haiku
there in them'. So, we are not observing them.~ 'Most of us are not
here, we would be, as Japanese practitioners put it, ~ook the time **to be**
the 'one moment'. Happily, we can LEARN, practice, ~ld BE in 'no mind'
pay attention better. ~ have our mind

Observing ourselves in action and, still, in non actio~ ~ilosophic,
psychology and spirit, in moment, becoming more interesting ~o ~uitful in
body, intellect, mind and heart. And thus increasing awareness ~o~ising,
leading to more acute sense-observations. And, perhaps, more m~ningful
haiku and senryu verses ?

All too theoretical, conjectural, notional? or something to be undertaken
and found practical and rewarding in our living? Until we, Beginners, try or
good experiences will remain in slumber?

Experienced practitioners report so many answers to Why write haiku
and senryu verses? as bringing us ways, opportunities to participate more
finely in living – and attaining wisdom.

We can receive deep perceptions, develop more striking insights, clearer
intuitions, all of which can through this poetry help answer many questions
about life and living today. Intellect which is our access to having the broader
view is more satisfied, through our experiences.

Again, we expand into a fresher, finer, more purposeful connection with
Great Nature – and our own nature! – and the yearly changing Seasons –
having an effect on our own personal domain and particular environments.

Overall, in our still and insightful moments, we write these verses, in this
ancient Japanese art of wisdom and brevity, while seeking a certain, fuller
glimpse of and into existence's ***Reality***?

Key Guidelines

...t) **Good** and (right) **Be careful of/ avoid**. This
Below, is line...elp Beginners' understanding and **best use of**
Table will hop...on (but no 'analysis').
questions and

...reading through these Guidelines, with a still mind, can
Us Begi...**al quiet assimilation of key guidelines** – and avoiding
take up a mental 'analysis'.
unprodu...

IF ...e ...**lways lively**) **mind** wants to 'analyse' something, then
'fall ...', ...ove onto next or another guideline, and **see what arises in**
'feeling...

The Table is shown on the opposite page:

Good	or	Be careful of/avoid
Show, just suggesting	or	Telling?
Concrete imagery	or	theorizing?
Image(s) from sensory perception	or	imaginings?
Sensory experience first	or	instant intellect!
One or more of the five senses	or	mind/intellect intrudes?
Something 5-7-5 is offered	but	is it expressed well enough?
Clear emotion expressed	or	strong but cloudy feelings?
Juxtaposition of two parts	or	one run-on sentence?
Can be said in one deep breath	or	not a natural flow?
Haiku's direct Season word	or	no direct focus on Nature?
Season word clear and helpful	or	'subtly' suggested and 'seen'?
Concise, precise image	or	too many words?
Few words, syllables, with balance	or	it has padding and is uneven?
Perception's present tense	or	just not immediate?
Clearly a direct experience	or	memory is faulty, not clear?
Reader can 'see', , 'imagine' clearly	or	too poetic, even fanciful?
Punctuation is helpful	or	is no punctuation better?
Depth of feeling generated	or	shallow, no shock or surprise?
Reader's sudden insight		Aha! Unambiguous, thought-provoking?
Perception/insight ambivalent	or	no clear Haiku image or reflection arising?
Verse is just 'unusual'	or	amazement, wonder?
Verse stands firm with meaning	or	just 'So What?'

'Season' as the 'soul' of Haiku?

Haiku is our personal experience of the reflection of Great Nature in verse form. It will encompass and show us What, When, Where that moment, that experience, was about, and open up 'why meaningful'. Long in Japanese tradition, spreading around the World since the 1900s, particularly since the 1920s in the 'West', it is short, brief, pithy, spoken in one breath, it is usually composed of three lines of 5, 7, 5 English syllables, the completed verse being of up to or as 17 English syllables. It is recognised verse poetry, with a seasonable or Nature reference in it, obvious or subtle. Season as the Soul of haiku? ANY (of our four annual) seasons relates us to great Earth Nature and helps give us an insight, reminder, into our natural, legitimate place on this planet and Galaxies and Universe.

'Haiku moments' heightened consciousness?

When well expressed, by experienced practitioners, 'Haiku moments' can capture and then reflect human perception through images direct from our senses during still and heightened consciousness. They might seem 'normal' at the time but, on reflection (unless passing shallow) can show us deeper meanings. This 'personal experience', direct experience, is held in subtle memory – NOT imaginings, which come and go, sometimes substantial, but never lasting. As one respected practitioner puts it: 'The good haiku will take the reader or listener directly to the 'Haiku Moment' and to the 'edge leaving them to 'fly'. By this I take him to mean 'connect with the inner meaning of what the composer/poet had seen and was speaking of in 5-7-5 below' ?

Follow the Guideline –
summer's heat or winter's snow:
let Season be shown !

Go beyond 'So What' response?

Three line, 5-7-5 syllabic disciplined verses might appear 'easy'. But too many (mine included) often bring forth a (disappointing) 'So what' response. I ask for us Beginners to — having got a semblance of our verse down, we look again and re-work till it is – apparently – close to the deeper 'perception' we KNOW is there, not 'first attempt, out on page. Gently, not mind, re-working. I ask us to really 'see' how from senses' inward gift of a 'perception', we come to see and appreciate that: the senses' work is done – the aware, awake 'perception' is embedded, slightly or deeply. We seek that it should re-appear in verse form. Stillness is required, body still, mind still – intellect the over-view, not necessarily imposing, just Witness. MIND provides the words, heart then brings the verse into being. For their must be emotion. And if there is true heart and emotion – the perception attains its purity. WE feel YES !

Sorry – the subjective trend in the West is towards away from the dignified human Self and Self-enquiry, and more towards artificial ego's dominance. Towards the more fanciful, surreal, abstract. A 5-7-5 approach might be a steadying influence, again? What perception might be asking: the deep point underlying this verse? What does Beginner find helpful in this text?

> Re-work, come closer
> to your deeper perception:
> Grace's inward gift

Our Work-in-Progress

This book is a Work-in-Progress. One thing is sure – no Beginner has to wear a straight-jacket of rigid rules; there are **some** – and the lengthy TABLE Questionnaire offers you — asks you, Beginner, to work hard creatively, and then question yourself — don't analyse. That approach locks in the inner-most creativity that lies within the emergence of haiku verses. It also in a way will handicap senryu which is writing reflecting man's limiting criticisms and foibles of us human beings; never really malicious!

As I've said, this offering is **a mix of General comment and Guideline help.** One wisdom I come back to came from a skilled practitioner, London based, whom I respect, has said, 'There is to be no intervention from the logical intellect'. After perception is lodged, the intellect holds the bigger picture, but does not interfere; productive mind brings forward the words necessary for the haiku or senryu to take final form. Remember the ancient counsel: break rules out of experience, not ego's inexperience or indulgence.

Repeating again: **Haiku in my original English verse**, as in this book, is deliberately three lines, 5-7-5 English syllables, of unrhymed poetic intent of directness, precision and clarity. It aims to reflect the essence of a moment experienced which has 'made its mark', internally. A brief moment, between perception embedded, and eventually realisation in verse-form; Realisation brought forth in writing, or reciting. It is YOUR 'seeing' life more deeply, more particularly – NOW. Making those 'moments' extra-ordinary from your recollection, reflection and writing. The reader or listener may be able to see or hear what you saw or heard either subtly or emotionally – extraordinary, really.

The practitioner's or poet's skill is just the 'clearing of the mirror' which is always there, surrounding us, though rarely appre. unless we are 'awake'.

You will 'translate' your Aha! Moment and experience **in your own words,** being careful to work against 'explanation'. 'comment' or 'interpretation'; **haiku is objective**, letting inner deeper meaning show itself to a still mind. Your own words and sensory images, in what is term 'concrete form', will be shared and delight readers and hearers.

Let creative flow —
use heart not 'analysis':
emotion's re-work

Memory is lit —
in mind's eye an image stirs:
words flow and Verse forms

Understanding more of What, Where, When

According to many experienced Haiku practitioners, there are three helpful, suggestive, crucial words the Beginner must understand and pay careful attention to: What, Where When.

The senses (when they are open, awake and observant – not lost in thoughts or dreaming) **brings to deepest mind** a perception (vivid or 'lightly passing'), from which a haiku/senryu may arise as **What.** The 'active' sense or senses here might be through the (subtle levels of) eyes (sight) or ears (hearing) smell, taste, and touch /feeling.

A specific place experienced, such as a local hill or mountain, or 'a clearing with an un-named pond', or our favourite pub can be **Where,** to our five senses.

'Season' is experienced as/in the time of the year. Something in Nature strikes us. Spring, summer, autumn, winter. And what they present through Nature, as well as human and other worldly activities in the environment; all or any Seasons can have their particular resonance to the practitioner or the Beginner. This is **When** One practitioner/author who impresses me enlarges this with Spring connects with haze and flowers peeping out; summer with clouds and bluer skies; autumn fog and dampness; and winter ice and snow, and bare tree branches.

> The 'rules' are but few –
> be clear why these three needed:
> all show 'resonance'
>
> All the year's Seasons
> Nature is awaking us
> saying 'See — not sleep'

What are your 'resonances'?

Haiku: Nature/Seasons

Summer is now passed,
misty autumn days appear –
cool stillness descends

Rain pours down on it,
this ancient oak no complaint:
wind, sun, snow – the same

I awake near dawn,
freezing early-winter night:
oh — surprise ! first snow

Visits tree often –
tweets tiny delicate song:
my mystery bird

Cold, cold winter's day,
in garden outside, I hear
his twitter's sunshine

The sun is rising,
its rays will come this way soon
to brighten my room

Eyes fixed on the screen,
tiny fly dances across –
my Lord, please not now

Love mother, father,
Earth, Nature, Source eternal:
this hard heart opens

You gave me this gift –
bag of luscious tomatoes,
pride of his home-grown

Her body is cold,
reflecting season's weather:
yet her heart so warm

Light fails, prayer calls,
precious bird outside obeys:
tweets its acceptance

Garden still and cold,
birds all tucked up in snug nests;
in earth, new life stirs

Nature's Earth says much,
little of wisdom is valued:
all need Divine's help

Bonfire Night again –
'protect all our animals' !
and old pensioners

Where are you, dear son?
Which travel location now:
in sunshine or snow?

Sitting, quiet room,
memories begin, flood in:
seasons, years lessons

Slowly, it passes,
silently, this winter night
as sleep evades him

How do we greet it ?
Season's Christ'ian festival:
truth's pleas – hearts open?

On a moonlit night,
walk with Nature, quiet mind,
oh! where are car keys?

He's older, slower.
Seasons pass so much faster:
lifespan's end closer

Truth asks straight of us –
world round me: see illusion?
warm sunshine helpful

He alights on branch
small bird outside, observant:
no tweet – joins me: still

I walk quite slowly
small plain patio:
such sunlight pervades

Awaken early,
'Great Universe' enlightens:
first, we are 'Starman'

Ah! first Winter snow,
deeper than forecast – poor birds:
so quiet outside

On many levels
within great Nature we 'know'
it tells us, seek more

Winter's such coldness,
it delights with snow, snowmen:
plus fresh air, brisk walks

Natural bare sight:
Not a leaf – my blossom tree;
spring's coverings soon

A grey day outside;
the sun still shining on Earth –
on the other side

Our ways we must change
climate change is so fearful?
The rain will still fall

You ask for hearing
you shy, delightful small bird —
you tweet me again

Wide eyed innocence
In the warm summer sunshine:
little girl's happy smile

Glorious full moon,
ice crystal sparkle on grass:
hard frost emerging

Flow'ring yesterday –
some blossoms dropping today:
season moving on

A red-breast swoops in,
takes but one look – he flies off :
I wanted to talk

She creates 'garden',
plants favourite seeds, grass grows:
Nature opens buds

New day, mind brightened
sun already shines hotly –
one step outside porch

Sunshine or rainy,
flowers open and stoic:
they welcome either

When the Season smiles,
we of course enjoy, smile too:
such sad Winter's day

Looks on in askance –
fat pigeon snatches HIS bread:
tiny red robin

He praises the seasons;
Spring, Summer bloom, Autumn, fade:
knows, honours Nature

New day, mind brightened
sun already shines hotly –
one step outside porch

Innocent creatures
pangolins live — no defence:
humanity's shame

He feels young again,
and recalls very first time:
snow deep as himself

Beneath earth, they grew
winter months and snow pass by:
spring flowers break out

Old English cottage,
his present delight outside:
roses cling, climb walls

It's soaking my face –
rain becoming heav'ier:
umbrella at home

Nature will share much
science unravels secrets –
humility's key

Nature and its laws:
both rule an aware soul's day;
season then season

> The day feels mournful -
> he trudges slowly to work
> in fitful sunshine

it's sweeping soft rain –
just what garden needs, she feels
from her dry indoors

> Large pot of flowers –
> colours vary, mild to bold:
> Nature's? no, hand-made

Stillness within room;
winter's day silent outside:
reflects silent mind

> Four Seasons changing,
> Nature, far too generous:
> snow, ice, bitter cold ?

Tree branch scrapes window!
too close ! my bus jerks to halt –
new buds look healthy

This universe awe:
many poets softly say
'See true miracle' !

This eve'ng observed:
mind still, yet so unsteady;
whom, where, can help trust ?

Walking out of door,
half-asleep, warmly greeted
today's true sunshine

No pen, no paper –
Nature is still, before him
just trusts memory

His deep sleep over,
arousal just at Sunrise:
silence, no bird-song

Your gentle sweet tweet
captures my early morn heart
asking for hearing

This gri winter's day,
light powd'ry snow hats about:
Oh ! not forecast yet

World dying slowly ?
We in midst 'Man-made' drama?
Nature just moves on

Lone yellow flower
hangs over this wood fencing,
scent woos passing girl

Morning's hot sunshine
so early this year, one thinks:
Spring's surprise entrance

Sunset in splendour –
in his contemplative mind
wonder is valued

He draws back curtain –
morning sunlight is absent;
sighs: grim autumn day

Flow'ring last day
some blossom dropping today
life ever moves on

Green and well tended,
lush garden's law a delight:
Nature adds caress

Autumn daylight fades
body nearly day older:
no mind's-twilight, yet

It, my small bird, back: –
others quiet — it tweeting
thank you, tiny friend

Cold New Year outside
perceptions from Nature bow –
'till walk's body warms

Thou in some distress,
low in thy eye 'Seasons' worth?
your Goodness is His

Its beauty immense
flashes, brief held, do not stay
Milky Way's jewel

Peaceful New Year's start –
for most – others' disasters;
Nature in two minds

Soft light gentleness
dusk's diff'rent garden appears:
flowers, plants, love it

My friends returning,
from lunch, hot sun, but cheery:
insights, by car, seen

When becomes too large ?
our trees over small pat'io
block out tea-time chat

Cold, senses aware –
Nature sits on my shoulder
make a walk across fields

My sleep to awake
this day – but like others not:
missing – tweets are back

Birdsong from outside:
mind and heart feel joyfulness –
Nature is One-ness

Walking, mind falls still,
senses are sharply open –
inward perceptions

Oranges, lemons
'life-like' on printed tea cloth:
I dry both the fruits

Such a graceful mess:
Seveal tour their garden;
they honour Nature

Summer rain drizzles
my tree outside is soundless:
birds shelter songless

That sweet winter tweet –
on tree outside flat, often;
what small bird? – all birds !

Cause which gives effect –
In seed, I see not now's tree:
divine consciousness

Riding a good horse,
whatever the year's Season:
trust is confidence

Peaceful New Year's start –
for most – others' disasters;
Nature in two minds

Soft light gentleness
dusk's diff'rent garden appears:
flowers, plants, love it

Wonderful sharp day !
he works outside, forgot gloves:
Ouch ! fingers are numb

They live 'well aware'
Nature's cunning animals:
caring Game-keepers

They both rule his world,
season following season :
Nature and its laws

My summer visit,
her garden greets again with
colourful clusters.

Rain-filled clouds gather –
then sev'ral thund'rous warnings:
wet sausages, *please* ?

Previous day's dirt
as though never been:
night's heavy rain

Nature's dominance:
It's a <u>*benign*</u> Source: –
why give, punish us?

Wet weather ignored –
my day has been so *inside;*
Nature ignores, too

I'd love to say it –
today, there's too much sunshine!
naïve …. ii has gone !

Dark before dawn breaks
ordering my groceries:
oh ! sun has risen

Splashes face, soft rain;
Nature replenishment gifts:
crop fields, gardens — thanks

Season and season —
They lead his everyday
Nature and its laws

Bloom in Spring, fading
flower-beds honoured daily
his brisk walk to work

Shared love – in cold frame !
my love, she peers in, exclaims !
their care, skills honoured

His life for others –
one still insight shows him clear:
yes, some help, much missed

'Foreign' territ'ry
one runs off, others they chase:
a nightly, Cats' squall

I'm told look around'?
when in awe I seek Nature.
I do, find mySelf

Sun's rays so searing
Plants when well watered, love it !
Crockety hat's shade

Sun gladdens pat'io,
birds give residents welcome
except sad house-bound

There is such wonder –
sunset in all its glory :
a still, quiet mind

Many garden trees
though stately, grow much too large:
scare off ev'ning sun –

Her artful soft lights
magical garden at dusk:
plants have striking 'stage'

We do ask, I'm sure –
both winter's cold, summer's heat ?
Who crafted the idea?

Blossom in the wind
Is returning to the bough ?
No, 'tis butterfly

Winter light fading,
the room's curtains are both drawn:
day's end, ev'ning comes

Just why so alone?
fissured, twisted, wounded bark:
you sweet chestnut tree

From seeds to giants.
Redwoods.Sequoias:
flourish together

Gnats in their thousands,
swirl about in close circles:
Summer heat promotes

Passing them each day,
flowers' beauty, seasons' change:
Spring *bloom*, Autumn *fade*

Classical statue
child's food offering on lips:
this grateful sparrow

This pigeon 'waddles'
one-two, one-two, ungainly :
ah ! but flying grace

Silent kitchen sees
Nature, his mind starts thinking:
be still, says Nature

They hope for a nice day,
walk, to remember his death,
it but rains and rains

Garden disappears,
patio lights on at dusk:
darkness claims beyond

Pensive, he ponders –
ego in man, Nature none:
for students — poser !

Warm day, some sunshine
as bus passes hospital,
clouds, illness shadows

NATURE does so rule us:
dispute this you may, but how?
We KNOW *(not)* LAWS Source ?

Body *(mere 86 years)*, powers down;
Seasons pass – body lessens
Nature...so honoured

Nature, under Law,
needs no clear absolution L
kill, be killed... NOT Man

It's been a grand day
with close friends – such heartfelt thanks,
I retire to bed

'Crawling' not for them –
Nature's 'climbers' go upwards:
they know 'transcendence' ?

Her flowers reflect
loving soft ev'ning sunshine –
we shared same feeling

We souls and Nature
see, obey Law: together?
or ...... consequences

Slow, 'my' awareness,
this garden's Nature speaking:
'This now I do need'

Ah ! to hot, to cold
all seasons acceptable
Nature so lawful !

Season's food the gift –
how to thank Nature fitly?
See it clear, in thanks

Nature ignores me?
I half miss them, our Seasons:
truth: half honours you

So stark, bare branches;
blossom tree winter sadness –
Oh ! joy's welcome soon

Reading, noticing –
stronger wind gusting through trees:
waves crash harbour wall

Ah ! they're here once more –
daffodils awaiting warmth:
early Spring yellow

Flowers in glass jar –
primary colours ablaze !
no.....artificial

Dagger beak flashes;
body still, below cascade:
grey heron's lunch

A sunset's splendour:
wonder's natural moment –
contemplative mind

It cloudy today
noticed, as my day goes on
reflects in my heart

Everyday/Senryu

Sincere compliment
'Thanks for eighty years service'
his extracted tooth

All this seeped in soul
slowly, gathered, there was truth:
I could not ignore

'Fairy-tale' Princess?
Her long-held dream was shattered:
'Duchess' not same thing

I awoke... so cold !
Nothing stirred, no tweet outside:
window left open

Twenty-first birthday,
four generations present:
loud but stilted talk

Oh gosh – I feel squashed;
my airline seat tight this flight:
the waistline fuller ?

No booze for patients –
necessary heavy rules?
thirst's desires stymied

Royal hearse drives by them,
the horses' heads tossed and bowed:
respect for the Queen

It resonates
I was to the truth so helped
sincerity such

Our perceptions deep
from whence we know not, they come:
shallow mind not Source

Picture before me:
It's Red Robin — touches heart
'Thank you for your Card'

They don't cry, hearts full,
practical believers know:
Witness is aware

Mind still— it appears
that which *arose all day*:
trust, be still: answer

Everyday insights
are granted, more to help serve
through mind being clear

All raucous laughter,
happy eyes and swirling hair:
girls at one! night out!

Crisply Ironed shirts,
they hang, in close ranks, on rails:
'soldiers' inspection

He longed to coach them –
'ladies' soccer team, South Wales:
too late — someone else

Lovely, vivacious –
she admits not listening
giggles 'so sorry'

My kitchen waste-bins
'seen' before; this 'memory':
reflecting my mind !

It looked outwards, then
those young days: 'Professional'
speed, strong….. not enough !

They promised, they came:
neighbour 'mechanics' open –
meals wheely flatpack

Silence and stillness–
no movement in audience:
absorbing lecture

Holdall is packed full;
one last item to squeeze in –
last item — get lost!

It rings out sincere;
African group, English church:
such joyful singing:

I look around think
'You here are so 'out of place.'
No —be still, seek truth !

He became famous —
tunneller key to escapes
he died underground

Oh ! 'racism' claimed —
black woman, strong, successful
missed positive goal

'Business' too far?
'Waitress-girls' so much exposed:
dignity second

Three diff'rent photos
Individuals so close —
Showing old to young

It clicks — these not mine;
so hard the work's words on truth:
whence comes this knowledge ?

Almost meeting up –
loving son offers visit:
common cold strikes !

Spring's magic welcomed —
daffodils smile us beauty
Alzheimer drug too

My patio small –
outside, in the Sun, rising :
Peace unlimited

Each day brings glimpses:
Nature entices senses:
'Please see my splendour'

How man/God govern?
What are those 'right principles'
Why do they exist?

So grateful your help,
Old Fogey appreciates:
free generous time

'Many'…. no answer –
in your bookful of Verses,
ONE may open heart

Upholds our friendship –
we both went on this journey
fifty years ago

He ponders, agrees :
'Doddery' word he now knows:
Welcome, my old age !

Each day brings glimpses;
Nature entices senses –
'please see my splendour'

Such untidy mess —
his desk again overflows:
speaks state of mind clear

Past moments relived,
imaginings, true or false
for faint memories

Quality of life?
How long will I likely live?
No ! Live it better.

In bus'ness – no fool;
as would-be Haiku poet –
'all over the shop' !

Pleasant polite talk,
old tensions aware noted !
lunch, old colleagues :

His old frail mother,
elderly son, suffering:
still, kiss on forehead :

My 'construction crew':
competent neighbour ladies:
bedroom clothes rails

China's New Year, such
delight in London's Soho:
five hundred lanterns –

Quiet hour musing:
sev'ral friends of Fifty years
where did it go right !

> Your words, Sir, gracious —
> but praise ! please, wait 'til I'm dead,
> 'Past' takes new faces

Is useful….. ego' –
plays key parts: — no Shakespeare fool,
helps show insight's truths

> What means poetry?
> yes, short verse might open truth
> e'en then, mind struggles

In restaurant life
whether vegan or beef steaks:
surrender to Source

> Telling me for weeks:
> computer's indigestion?
> But I, words-only

There is link intact:
we smile often though apart
cartoon cards meet need

Telling me for weeks:
computer's indigestion?
I clueless, ploughed on

Hundred volunteers –
generosity's hallmark
re-house disabled

Their frugality –
he does not get offered rise:
new horizons now

They're often bad guide:
off'ring such coarseness, crudeness –
love films – not today's

Diff'rent actors 'work':
speech, silent mime — each delight
we glimpse truth in both

Upset – game's result:
she said they lost by a 'fluke'
Wise: 'life IS LAWS fair' ?

I will not make thing
but she demands not drop more
Ah ! scotch and soda

Inspired comes and goes –
sadness music Schubert knew;
hut rising HOPE too !

What means poetry?
yes, short verse might open truth
e'en then, mind struggles

In restaurant life
whether vegan or beef steaks:
surrender to Source

He's such loving dog
showers love on ev'ryone:
'Come please play with me' !

House-bound Pensioner
needs withdraw his cash, Bank's 'No':
views him ....'Profitless'

Pressure builds again –
it just cannot be contained:
a second loud sneeze !

Movement, sound, colour –
We're drawn, attention captured !
yet Screen silent, still

Dad's stick falls over –
it still has life of its own:
Yes, Dad – I hear you

Lovely Irish name !
Encompassed all I valued –
Married but score years

Patient listening.....
they hear her good sense wisdom:
she stutters softly

You, I — what a pair!
How we so much laugh and laugh :
those moments of truth

Sad ruined sight, sense-less –
village's one valued phone box –
who fire destroyed it ?

She speaks quietly
they wait on her wise counsel:
is it Yes? Or No?

Truth offered for all,
now given around the world:
from Ind'ia, Lord's wish

My worship honours —
missed, or but late, so often:
how can I ask Grace ?

Nuclear winter?
humanity underground !
courage is with them

Erupts far away –
The EU's five days to reach
Airlines ? just cancel

(Skilled practitioner):
final verse — ego praises?–
"you are so kidding!"

So accomplished, he ! —
notes flow, his speedy fingers:
music-lovers sigh

What's that ? the mind asks –
birds excitedly twitt'ring :
my ears, eyes seek cause

This is so boring !
disgruntled teenager moans:
while awaiting life

Her real name hidden
'Hallelujah' renowned:
guitarist supreme !

My night-time dreaming:
in still darkness of my bed
scenes full of colour !

cars by the hundred,
queue moves but few yards, horns blare!
such slow, slow lemmings

Mistake seen, regrets,
he's given a second chance:
dissolve ignorance?

Do see thinks straight, friends:
you applaud me as 'poet':
skills, but I refresh **honour**

Friends and my neighbours
are just not separated;
this home-bound needs all

Her real name hidden
'Hallelujah's' unity
guitarist supreme !

'Safety measures
demanded, but they ignored:
animal kills child

Table lamps light room,
screen gives light too, there to help:
his inward sight blind

War zone for so long,
now, its professional class
'refugees' abroad

'Magazine of Year
edited all-female staff:
bright young male tea-boy

Just surface worship
such slim legs, from here to there !
He prized good heart more

Box folders, books, tapes
and paperwork — busy room:
shelf willing helper

The mind wanders off,
and sight is trees, not the wood:
thinking's pathway fades

Begin to repeat –
It grates — noisy grass cutting;
would I him jobless ?

What is 'clear seeing'?
Tutor explains it's there, Truth:
but asks 'work for it'

Love and duty pair,
such kisses on her forehead:
our so frail mother

From small hand-held start,
they both became 'experts' fast
sons' first computers

Nature's beauty loved,
he's aware of human theft:
caretaker's new shed

We ask – good or ill?
un-natural way forward:
cattle mega-farms?

Replace cap on pen –
gently, or with such hard jab:
where is force subtle?

Yes ! arise, glitter
'jewelled words' poetic style:
can I see core's Truth?

So friendly a drink –
but no more than one champers:
easy to forget

Service holds not back,
ask more, when it's true service:
or 'they' mere 'numbers'

Amazing – here, NOW
each day an awakening:
make day practical

He is from the past,
our delight — wondrous talent:
beloved wall picture

Telephone book.... friends;
numbers go back, some decades;
still alive, still friends?

Long journey, first step —
no, common sense says — put off:
pouring down, just wait !

Mind and memory:
past returns into this life —
with discarded gaps

Ah! sizzles in pan,
appetite insists — a taste!
Wife hits hand away

Her frown disapproves,
sugar's two spoons, or just one:
warned, he hesitates

Sad, she's 'sectioned';
sev'ral come to 'collect her':
why smash her door down?

She admits to truth –
she's not good listener:
giggles her 'Sorry!'

Body in old age;
these eyes are not what they were:
still inward-subtle

I order one thing
one more …. I try your patience!
I should own own shop

He believes strongly –
fit, active embodiment;
shoulder's gone again !

Such distinctive noise !
my ancient car to dinner:
a sigh – gasket blown

She earns such high praise;
the deserv'd Award is her's:
our 'Cleaner of Year' !

My friend is expert –
honour to his 'knowledge':
he says….Verse 'So what' !

Fecund, It strikes him
means more than Nature's bounty:
his draft book finished !

Mind thinks on problem;
such a wondrous intellect:
problem is resolved

Country's governance –
he's not without his ideas:
struggles to 'sell' them

Her present to the World,
all seem to seek violence:
bunch of daffodils

Peace before outburst -
your views intend demonstrate:
peaceful senryu !

His skills are expert;
these Book-verses come alive –
hundreds start to speak !

How can I thank them !
my door: heart-open neighbours
I'm short just of bread

I thought that I loved
those desires proved no basis
her's did not meet mine

Champs Elysees Noir
from under Arc de Triomphe
gift of superb chocs

Thick growth around Book –
my words cut through – HIS sharper :
trust sword of logic

Philosophy/Psychology

Why do you say 'Sir'?
it is sincere bow to you –
for you ARE 'Tutor'

Both older, slower –
two souls working together:
moment of kinship

Finer behav'iour,
coarseness into refinement:
his living improves

The mind can offer
purity and clarity –
when silent and still

All have had sadness,
even tragedy in life:
with patient courage

It's such a puzzle –
humans have so many 'I's;
which rules me today?

Is it remembered,
in busy ev'ryday life:
dignity of Self

Words show me meaning,
perception feeds words slyly:
true source is Witness

Family heirlooms –
she makes light of them today:
those past centuries

In twenty-one words:
the world's seven great failings?
Ghandi spoke, I heard

With sight's clarity:
false way to open 'the Gate'–
here's no wine today

Both in heart know truth,
He and she, they wish to part;
end of their romance

You may ask, why one
Nature – God's Laws, they decide –
not us 'passers-by'

They bring into light
so, thus, words like 'perception':
for they mean 'wisdom'

'Mistakes' can appear
when 'my' attention wanders:
moment's 'truth' covered

Observed or perceived?
Senses sharp, clear or clouded:
Mind's memory's need

With sight's clarity:
false way to open 'the Gate'–
here's no wine today

Both in heart know truth,
He and she, they wish to part;
end of their romance

You may ask, why one
Nature – God's Laws, they decide –
not us 'passers-by'

They bring into light –
so, thus, words like 'perception':
for they mean 'wisdom'

We often forget –
Old age sometimes brings sadness
His eternal love

Example for all:
his look – attentive, list'ning;
'Hear your voice speaking' !

Distinctly diff'rent –
'striving and doing' so wrong:
just 'let it be done'

This is Age of vice,
ancient wise scriptures warn us:
consciousness covered

Young self worked long hours –
old age means 'productive spurts';
measure such great gift

It may well be true:
clearer view of 'perception'?
Direct knowledge touch

Blank white page, waiting;
this writing is joint effort;
I, nothing to say

Can this small-self 'I'
become mystic transcendent?
Unknowing unbeliever

This embodiment
when insight with clarity
serves best the 'Witness'

Old age imbalance:
philosophy asks 'No fear' –
yet false step means 'fall'

We see not…. not ONE
believe TWO our common state –
'transcendence', mere word

Rooms objects and thoughts;
lamplight us causing shadows:
his mood is dark too

He always says 'Sir'
with def'rence, to his 'better'–
meaning in THIS life !

Children's faces sad
tear at heart-strings at causes:
such world poverty

That our only path:
born to but strive and endure,
divine Grace – knowledge

'Seeing' in moment,
perception is 'stored':
'subtle' key opens

The workings of 'heart'
when truly known, praise the Lord,
bend knee, say I AM

Tutored, 'sees' the world,
yet how, dear heart, this each day
strength to obey Laws?

Food, mind, those desires:
how to rule such 'intruders' ?
believe they're NOT yourSelf

Ten thoughts are wasteful
whatever you value them:
One will honour Lord

Wisdom's guide –
me: fewer Blogger's tirades,
philosophy depth

Neighbour and I talked:
family members fall out?
Other ego's: mine?

In this older age,
it seems still quite natural
to welcome each day

Demeanour sincere
keeps open clear path to Truth
when asks: !, this life?

Senses lead insight
Perception, in us, joins One
needs mind to give words

Public speaker knows:
'Keep them with you, whatever'
be calm, no insults

Done, done, done..... and more –
Good morning's work Jobs just flowed –
'I' let things alone.

Poet feels no limits –
his connection can transcend:
aim nature's insight

A comment from you
awakens search question:
how insights arise?

> Present, quiet voiced,
> the wise leading, East and West
> known to seekers few

Missing no detail
before us all, all to 'see':
her unmoving gaze

> Old frailities change –
> Senses give fresh perceptions:
> Such insights then act

Why cannot I 'see'
what others 'see' so cleanly?
Mind not present, dreams

> His laughter lightens
> solemn moment understood:
> perception refined

Such surprise insight –:
original Verses flow —
this 'I' does nothing !

It is in us all –
yet ME separate, is claimed:
true knowledge can wait !

Man aims for the stars–
spends riches and lives getting there:
forgets SELF on way

Old age frailty
fanciful – I know Lord's Laws?
Ego is ruling

Our past can sap strength
in present doubts – but let's hold !
GOOD given freely ?

How does speech arise?
from deep within, wise explain
before that, Lord knows

I interviewed them
recorded their lives, looked back
honest: wins, failures

It will all dissolve
some believe; out of THIS life,
pain now — no pain then ?

My table's a sight —
Piled with masses of paper
No order — I slept

Ignorance prevails,
inhumanity results:
not Lord's wish nor Law

Such a scowling face —
unaware – unattractive?
Friendship not option

Softly then loudly,
gentle talk to pensioners:
'Can you hear me'?

Helping the leader?
often shrewder advisers
ideology limits

They are sent to help:
she refuses — door smashed down
She's sadly sectioned

Perceptions..... Witnessed !:
insight rises..... from memory;
senses 'see .....MIND'S words

We speak of its charms;
music's spiritual charms:
how little we know

Man aims for the stars –
spends riches and lives getting there:
forgets SELF on way

Old age frailty
fanciful – I know Lord's Laws?
Ego is ruling

Our past can sap strength
in present doubts – but let's hold !
GOOD given freely ?

How does speech arise?
from deep within, wise explain
before that, Lord knows

The brief moment 'seen',
'Perceptions' mind's mystery :
fewest 'words' mean much

'Substance' has many meanings:
substratum, Creator, Source
for us, answers 'inside'

Universe 'out there?
He ponders 'or inner us':
In, out – ONE with it !

Philosophy group's new talk
can Man live in unity?
History: Big Ask !

My friend, serious
How can we KNOW, be certain ?
Wise: Heart's smallest space

Shown to be so wrong,
what is our heart's reaction?
Concede YES ! Move on

Inside: hear mind, heart
wise steadfast in pure knowledge
'MY' says 'All say: One, Source, Lord'

Oh, mind, what nonsense !
Self does not take 'a day off'
You again, do sleep !

'Do wake up'.......I start....
Was it so, half minute since
my tutor's last words ?

YOU praise me? Not so
Souls around speak so wiser;
tempt none the ego

Inside: hear mind, heart
wise steadfast in pure knowledge
'All say: One, Source, Lord'

It's quite a question?
Logic and the human heart?
Emotion says One

'Do wake up'.......I start....
Was it so, half minute since
my tutor's last words ?

YOU praise me? Not so
Souls around speak so wiser;
tempt none the ego

Her slender form, prized;
haunts memory, prompts desires:
now, give up for truth ?

I, witness, there, heard:
her language not respectful –
HIS the bus servant

'No! I'll not Review'
YOU helped me so write this book ?
No, honour stands firm

Foot up, toe wriggles,
Body's living miracle
see, wave with yourSelf

Few indeed know this -
when Love's love so perseveres
the Gods are joyful

A very bright man,
yet, a cold disdainful snob:
inside, does he look ?

Buying in 'spare parts':
losing reality's touch,
'Celeb' women lead

A line of wood fence
challenge – not resistible !
lad leaps over all

She knows she's lost him,
he – no offer of return:
love now disint'rest

Fine ingredients ?
politics and principles:
is he a statesman ?

They ask, lazily –
'Why create' seeks clear answer:
the aim ? gift for all

Each day, mind questions;
I look out, dawn opens up,
what pond'rings today?

Sounds and noise frequent –
why does silence mean so much?
it is transcendence

This was written well !
Self-praise? Don't deny the Muse,
she will depart you

Heard and studied more:
with evidence, Grace transforms
into living knowledge

Journalists, authors drink
much, 'tis said; they venerate –
which, all, Nine Muses?

Scenes – children's faces,
happy, poverty unknown:
become aware – truths curse?

He acts the role tight,
from known the universal:
Script, love, and TRUTH

Does mind realise?
It creates little really:
thoughts arrive, leave soon

Life's school is open,
unending education:
try not to abscond !

Names down centuries –
his thoughts, sighs freely 'Honour':
great men and women

From her, cartoon card
reminding me to miss her:
apart, we both smile

Business prospering –
they spend much on staff comfort:
priceless goodwill banked

Sentencing himself,
keeping his love closed and weak:
lives in own prison

Guests as family –
so loving warm atmosphere:
thriving bed-breakfast

Some warn of decline –
how measured, in our lifestyles?
'We want it ALL.....NOW !

Why is it, I ask —
she can't see MY qualities !
Ego speaks too loud?

It startles again —
innocence and peace-aware:
this (my) child's still eyes

She plays half her heart:
taught thus, Godly music more
not 'conformity'

My words come from still,
I ask you, student, HEAR still:
wise words float away

Me, City soul
her 'great' safaris...
what other I 'wimp' ?

They brush off cleric's words
God, mammon — YOU follow which!
denial's closed minds ?

YOU 'see' – understand –
such horrid disappointmentl
life, to my mother

Old frailities change –,
semses give fresh perceptions:
such insights then act

Ev'ryday, at some time
memory brings him himself:
not when World insists

Senses look outward –
report back inward:
Memory's myst'ry

MY working manner
is heart OR mind, conflicting;
one, other, shut up

Still disappointment –
how do we leave illusion:
gain reality?

Strike first, hit them hard:
a wise heart believes other –
force is not love's arm

From deep within us
insight's broad brush strokes' picture:
careful words refine

Enjoyable lunch –
he ponders, lifestyles diff'rent:
glimpses in minds' eyes

image shared, in flash –
they are both moved tasting words,
poet and reader

He speaks easily,
possibly not mere thinking?
Essence from within

Ponders paths offered:
enlightenment? touch will do!
No – all or nothing …..

Why do I question?
For mind to demand 'Answers' ?
Cosmos is not child

Sharpness I welcome -
this Director cuts and cuts:
his aim – Be Awake !

We meet: glass of malt,
enjoy those moments *Present* –
my friend, the neighbour

That golden voice stirs,
promises hidden virtues:
her perfect mask slips

A dark age, Mankind?
To most, theory not real:
pride is high, truth low

Do look more, talk less –
he can't see her qualities
ego shouts too loud

We strive, happy, sad,
achievements glitter and pass –
what is permanent?

Wisdom's words show us:
source of our greatest power ?
Seek knowledge inside

Great truth speaks, impacts;
his great words….. beyond the War:
ALL who heard – *hearts* moved

Practical Philosophy ?
Viable, this confused AGE ?
You ask Hugh Jackman

They read them aloud –
he Haiku, she the Sonnets:
their East-West concord

His heart knows better –
mind sinks … winter's loneliness ?
conscious knowledge stirs

Senses collect much;
from memory, perception:
mind's words make picture

Mind thinks on problem;
such a wondrous intellect:
problem is resolved

Country's governance –
he's not without his ideas:
struggles to 'sell' them

A worthy search – truth;
the words, but not the practice?
Philosophy' words

I blink just the once –
that moment Creation turned
I start again

Good minds think it through,
true judgement then will prevail:
Haiku wisdom speaks

Spirit

When 'thank you' is due
to whom do I offer it?
mySelf as the Source

Irish ancestors,
re-birth eternal law spoke:
new body is Welsh

Happiness for all –
Gift offered for our living:
The Lord's Nature's Will

You are me, I you?
embodiment asks question:
soul is the answer

Soul with a question,
through this mind, body and heart:
YOU Lord me, I you?

It is there, then it,
moment, as quickly, is gone:
trace of sublime bliss

Goodness and goodwill
shines, glows, on her outer face,
bliss pervades inside

Walking by window,
two compassionate-carers
her large-hearted help

Insight's clarity?
false way to open 'the Gate':
no red wine today

Woman's face, sleeping,
man's face, intent, watching her:
her inner strength's both

She fell in courtyard,
I heard, did not hear, her cries:
silent calls still haunt

She fell in courtyard,
I heard, did not hear, her cries:
silent calls still haunt

Walking by window,
two compassionate-carers
her large-hearted help

Mankind surprises –
We marvel selfless spirit
Not bounteous Source

Search and you will find,
the Messiah's promised words:
my Lord: mine own Self

Being in 'OneSelf''
seems such a mystical goal:
obey wise with *faith*

Permanent Witness !
I concede that my Lord's Law
needs no Self defence.

Why is it? That when
'I' sit, let Haiku arise,
the feeling is of 'bliss'?

Eat out of saucepan,
If you in such weakness must –
offer it to Lord

Your vinegared mind –
belief in Nature's honey
sweetens outward love

He loves son freely,
asks just one 'gift' in return:
share more of yourSelf

Where does it come from ?
Belief, trusting heart, honour:
source – ONE Source, my heart

THIS is well retired
age eighty-six: what comes now?
Trust – HIS Law knows best

IT comes to haunt me,
recounting ways I failed:
live next life truer

How can I know you
unless I concede to truth:
you are my own Self

My true conviction –
what was hidden is now clear,
heart-felt gratitude

Our lifestyle feeds flies ?
Lower creatures, to become ME?
Soul's source: 'Do not kill!'

He hates, swats flies –
such a troublesome edict:
they have a soul, yours

Wise teachings tell us,
each soul in its current life,
is part of Oneness

What is it, in us
which we do not create?
Holy, silent words

'Visions': word too strong:
obey insight's disciplines
they reflect Truth's truths

A thank you, my Lord,
just body's break: a sandwich,
in mind's calm. thought YOU

Once I turn to Light,
All becomes even clearer
'My' truth's aim enhanced

Rules, with care, broken –
Justice honourably served:
Spirit/Law decides !

Some beliefs say thus –
there is void in heart's centre:
how, for 'I AM' there?

The workings of 'heart'
when truly known, praise my Lord
bend knee, and say 'I AM'

Embodied voice speaks:
carries with it the Lord's Will;
HIS not mine…. Finer

Body is older,
heart is wiser, I but trust ?
read Good Book – think YOU

Best she knows in him
she can't give heart's praise:
what is barrier?

Inner light shines
ignorance cover weakens:
others benefit

Wisdom's words, from saints
are flowing into us now:
why me so stilling?

These such brief Verses
can open transcendence path:
WITH mind's quiescence

In body's stillness,
In mind's deep'ning quietude, :
rest... AND ... transcendence

Mind part to play, later
these Verses, perception key:
from SELF, then need WORDS

Marvellous life, this –
that sublime is not captured
older may live on

Awake, remembrance:
consciousness is NOW,
and I am NOW THAT

Senses unruly –
turbulence sweeps the mind off:
there is still witness

Still see inward clear:
but eyes just not what they were:
body enters old age

Many friends buried
now, un-morbid, he wonders,
lifespan….Grim Reaper !

Spiritual friend –
Forty years touch seldom
In heart always

A 'thank you' is said –
trust: for-to whom do I pray?
teaching says 'yourSelf

I make assertions
firm belief in my insight !
Tutor, gently: No !

THEY have found this Way
into the Source, ancient truth':
third eye may…..open

What was THAT regret?
soccer ladies coach:
they never asked me !

Source's Will, through me –
sometimes, clear, often muddled:
may Grace intercede

Bread falls from the table
recovered, bless-ed, eaten:
dignity for Lord

Rich and sonorous,
the meditation deepens:
until silent *Home*

I write down with care:
mem'ry needs Source's Witness –
good sleep insight's aid

She obeys good ***nous***
acts natural, and ignores
man's silly rulebook

Asked about 'Universe',
something ancient shines in him?
Spirit's wisdom's lamp

When confusion reigns,
day's demands cause disarray:
seek the One within

Such beautiful soul
shines and brighten all who meet –
touched indeed by Grace

The view is much changed
his 'inner belief' deepened:
Unity's wholeness

Practical or memory?
what is it, to remember ?
Source, seasons, all flows

I might say 'I love'
In truth, can it be for sure:
for I know not mySelf

More drink, self alone?
No, Lord, we're never alone
YOU 'see' stopper

The view is much changed
his 'inner belief' deepened:
Unity's wholeness

Practical or memory?
what is it, to remember ?
Source, seasons, all flows

Spirit's light within –
Succours and warms open heart:
Lit by Consciousness

More drink? self alone?
No, Lord, we're never alone
SELF puts the cork in

His project goes well
aware quiet compan'ion
is but Grace, himself

We need be open;
this afternoon is wasted?
Great things, no? humbled !

Souls who *are* seeking;
those souls *near* seeking;
some 'something *missing*'?

> In 'opening up'
> I am hearing, and speaking
> to myself, list'ning

That moment of truth
'Maybe it ain't our bus'ness':
West's sad saying, today

> Solemn moment, church:
> 'my soul, my soul', it rises;
> What, inside, I know ?

LAW sees souls 'shining'
or souls so 'clouded over' :
fee; absolutely safe?

> Imagination
> can foster ego's conceit:
> true SELF witnesses

Meditation's path
verse-images flood his mind:
Oh ! not this, not this

She still seeks solace
though sure, trusting in spirit
year ago, he died

New day dawns brightly;
I rise, heart opens grateful;
life's beauty again !

Perceptions so deep
she so guarded keeps within:
confined inner world

Guilt-less, shopping mall
violence sees souls depart:
twisted Faith, hate speaks

We worship God or small self:
something falls quiet?
desire leads – know Truth

Strange ideas all,
Islamic cleric's belief:
debauched cause earthquakes

Insights arising,
particularly good day:
spirit remembered

Mantra sounds but once,
then disappears whence its Source:
wise sure – it's yourSelf

Their music gripping
almost alien, some felt:
emotionless hearts

Day's events ended,
merit? demerit?
Law rules – go to sleep

He gives son freely,
lovingly asks but one gift:
"Share more of yourSelf"

This, our existence
can well be 'timelessness dream':
life's time-clock ticking

Some times, each day....jab
'not regular Church-goer'?
Worship – no limit

One in friendship shrinks –
she seeks spiritual talk:
his....SO practical

On the screen.... surprise !
'characters' come so alive:
dialogue's clear *'truth'*

Suffering's heart's cry:
Oh ! would this life's pain stop now
We, not Lord's Laws,fail

Gentle, so was I:
yet physio saw....'body'
not 'spirit' present

What is clear 'seeing'?
available.... *but unclear*:
truth, you must want it !

On her slow deathbed,
many times, I looked into her eyhes
found there both our loves

In this one moment,
a frisson? or unity:
Group experience

Wise say 'Great is Son'
In evr'yday living, so:
Lord loves both our souls

Seasons now pass slow,
yet! each Season..... glimpse Truth;
yes ! Lifespan end close

A friend, such a friend:
qualities, such loving faith:
only Lord's Source knows

I'm busy....later !
Lord's Law notes; Witness still:
yet heart pleads 'forgive'

> The heart opening,
> mind seeks more refined knowledge:
> until contentment

It's there – no intent:
critical in mind and mouth:
break spirit's wise lines

> Each has a pure heart
> the wise explain 'What goes wrong?'
> no need 'transcendence'

Answers are sought, but
questions put half-heartedly:
sincere in striving!

> Indeed, we understood more –
> *THAT* suffuses our meeting:
> as Consciousness flowed

Existence, he feels,
is pointless, timeless dreaming:
world's clock is ticking

Somewhat my feelings?
I see the leaves dropping –
It's such a tired rose

When 'me' is in sight
wisdom says ignore –
it covers but truth

When it arises,
wish to retire to my bed:
from world? join with Self?

They pass my window,
two large ladies conversing –
compassion's Carers

Senses when subtle
I know little of it all:
what Witness records

What joy I do feel,
this period in life good:
now and day ahead

These passing moments
important – and I awake:
no perceptions lost

This *creative* work,
resting in contentment's Source
perceptions emerge

Wisdom touched them both:
failed marriages – not again!
Thirty year friendship

Clarity to 'see' ?
available but unclear !
Truth awaits true need

By his gentle love
he shows her she is beloved:
how to prove One-ness?

Time is precious –
her end of life prognosis;
she lives in the Present

The wise, they tell us:
'We pass through life many times' –
'Truth always with us'

An untidy mess –
his desk is overflowing:
state of mind disclosed

Oldsters mourn to me
'quality and standards rare' !
Nation's dismal state

Now twenty five years
still more to know of themselves:
this live-out bonding

He's very bright man
but a cold disdainful snob:
always lived alone

Such a sad ruined sight
that gang's fire had swept through it:
phone box to repair

Dominion dispute –
one runs off, other chases:
cats' ownership squall

When you know her well:
beauty outside, inside too,
soul full of delight

His 'work-in-progress' –
it does not go all that well:
questions his beliefs

Changeable weather –
the Snow outside has come, gone:
Nature's iffy mood

Fat-living departs
financial diet imposed:
they join street riots

Church room so pleasant –
large, airy ad, welcoming:
His silent Presence

Summer rain drizzling,
not a sound from tree outside:
birds shelter song-less

When I speak 'MY' truth
my limits is become plain:
untruth can hide well

There's one thing, my Lord,
of your Grace – to ask of you:
please bless these Verses

We struggle to KNOW
and SEE, but yet so cloudy
we know, see, here, now

When spirit moves us,
we ask and clouds move away:
there is the Sun again

Potpourri

Potpourri is a mixture of scented dried flower petals or a collection or a medley or a miscellany.

Welcome, *all Beginners – a challenge for you below. You will choose, you will decide. Your enjoyable task is to read **any** Verses, in this Potpourri Section, and **identify them**, in your new understanding as:*

NATURE/.SEASONS, or

EVERYDAY/SENRYU, or

PHILOSOPHY/PSYCHOLOGY or

SPIRIT

The author advises that, though well checked, some Verses may have 'slipped through' as not quite 5-7-5 and not 17 English syllables (maximum).

No answers are provided by the author, as there is such a thing as a 'hybrid', a Verse which might not find a home under any Section.

Please enjoy testing and 'honing' your new skills!

Such moments treasured,
when insight both sees and knows:
gift the Muse presents

Would you ask Great Chef
to poke the barby?
yet father, grandson do

Few know this indeed
when love's love so perseveres
the Gods are joyful

Coos is boasting or lonely,
or seeking mate?
Does HE really know?

Time is precious –
her end of life prognosis:
she lives in the *Present*

From so deep inside
that small secret place all know:
yourSelf – *there* is home

Alone, and his life,
living and future destroyed
refugee's 'what more'?

Short man, four by four,
the big dog almost his size:
stroll amicably

Twisted hatred speaks
in our cheerful shopping mall
violence seeks deaths

Not dentist again?
help I do not want but need -–
a tooth's painful cry !

Brassy horn bugles
accordion supports it –
so sad their street tune

Silent, dignified,
awaiting service – insist:
her modest wood chest

'You are JUMPING us –
me and queue all criticise !
she... on diff'rent bus

He 'sees' as others
knowing she values silence,
tongue is ordered

Her home-grown meal
Its sunshine vegetables
heart can but shine too

Sorrow's heart sinking
awakes from their drugs
she smiles at me

Awake clarity
from cancer's drugs she struggle:
her smile was alive !

From perception comes picture
mind helps, presents subtle words:
subtle more subtle

Whisky opens me
Not true on so many counts
rather, truth second

Each day she bows to
Nature's gen'rous abundance:
often to its Source

This esteemed author
such penetrating insights:
Ah, yes, those ladies

He remembers well,
the horror, there once again:
the bullets, they flew

What is happening?
those birds twitter hoisily –
attention flies to cause

She sighs so often –
He is coughing and sneezing:
Yeti-like coldman

How does he end this?
In her eyes adoration:
unjustified love

With cautious, cool smile,
her talk is so clipped, reserved –
compassion is rare

Their annual lunch –
goodwill – and *spirits* ! abound
jovial jokes loud

Early Spring afternoon –
cloudy sun shows, garden still:
life beneath moving

Sunday stroll for them,
girl on horse passes, careful:
polite 'good mornings'

Blandishments ignored,
he questions all on wisdom:
Socrates and truth

All life passing it
ever watchful in window:
china dog, sad eyes

Theirs, modest small house
on front paving, so proudly:
large, expensive car

Deep untouched inland,
Indian tribe discovered
film's poignant script touched

To Iceland she went
famed Northern Lights were missing:
they showed **in U K** !

Does the drunken poet
mirror ancient drunk sailor?
both stagger – land, sea

This train, why so fast?
I miss slow Countryside look;
speeding daffodils

Ghostly images
emotions arise unbid:
mind do so behave !

Bond and share a bed,
life's latest traumas arise:
can love bring them peace?

When this good tutor
seeks, entices their 'answers'
truth beyond ego's

Admired physical –
losing reality's touch –
'Celebs' buy-in spares

Mind seeks always more,
I sit here in the Present:
WILL tells it – be still!

Her present to the World,
all seem to seek violence:
bunch of daffodils

Peace before **outburst** –
your views intend demonstrate:
peaceful Haiku !

His skills are expert;
my Book-verses come alive –
hundreds start to speak !

Nuclear winter?
humanity underground !
Lord's spirt with them

Her present to World,
such is violence around :
bunch of daffodils

Sixty-ith today !
their wedding bells long ago
friends' fish-chip supper !

Peace before **outburst** –
your views intend demonstrate !
OR peaceful Haiku !

His skills are expert;
my Book-verses come alive –
hundreds start to speak !

Nuclear winter?
humanity underground !
Lord's spirit with them

Memory is lit -
in mind's eye an image stirs:
words flow and Verse forms

It cloudy today
noticed, as my day goes on
reflects in my heart

Busy... then look out –
my winter no longer there:
outside sunny Spring

I blink just the once –
that moment Creation turned
I start again

Her present to us,
when all seem seek violence:
bunch of daffodils

That seen insightful:
perception's inner meaning
often remains hidden

Mind's eye sees the words
in Haiku's Five-Seven-Five:
known still stays unsaid

His skills are expert;
my Book-verses come alive –
hundreds speak to you !

Nuclear winter?
humanity underground !
Lord's spirit with them

He ponders once more -
so quickly Verses arise
reflect not heart's aim

In short-Verse visions
Beginner feels such meaning
now begins practice

Peace before outburst -
your views intend demonstrate:
peaceful Haiku ?

End Thoughts

WE humanity ARE Nature everyday
yet we also transcend it, if that is our WILL

Greetings – so this literary journey of discovery has come to its end as a **Work-in-Progress,** in which I've included much repetition (hopefully a good thing for Beginners' eventual assimilation).

The experienced purist practitioners show us how they, expertly, compose and write Haiku and Senryu. They explain the enjoyment and benefits to them – and maybe to us – in composing/writing of Haiku Verses, and the uplifting role that such verses and insights they can bring to our everyday living.

There are few articles, understandably, which, easily, try to explain haiku and senryu in terms of how it all — perceptions, insights — arise in us (we humans are SO notoriously changeable, mind attention spans so variable-viable, often undisciplined beings). How also there is ever-available brilliance and productivity in us (as well as a verse's failed So What?) How this is closely shadowed by our not 'knowing' ourselves, deeply.

Just as we may ask why? write and read and study gentle and pleasant and often startling insightful haiku, and devise mischievous senryu particularly, so after several revealing, useful experiences putting us in the spot when we might ask 'Whence does our momentary flash of perception and intuition come from, leading to such inside knowledge'? Does it arise from personal temperament or a metaphysical inner source, or When, rather, from intellect and mind, perform rather routinely OR under one Will's discipline. Can we or how can we, put ourselves/ourSelf in place or position, favourable condition or environment, to generate such amazing (or ordinary) verses?

The big question:

> ➢ do the so-important 'concrete' images in a good meaningful haiku or senryu —

> ➢ depend on our connection with subtle world mental dimension, or a 'Muse'?

However speculative or exploratory the above, I'm sure other rational, reasonable explanations and viewpoints can be proffered, are indeed offered by experienced practitioners. But for us Beginners, all above are for another author, another book.

Let's end by considering **'image' (clear, strong, subtle or 'passing')** Revered pioneers in past decades have reminded us that the verses speak about our experiences in images via and from the senses, of such perceptions being directly and with intensity formed **in memory** and intellect, and in one momentary experience, from **acute observation** of Nature (and human nature).

What is an image? One contributor to the Internet, a decade ago, trying to take his students beyond the 5-7-5 'limitation' and into the incorporation of 'creative imagination', **sees it as being Pictures arising from and in your thoughts, which can encompass from (subtle) sight, hearing, smells/scents, taste, feelings/emotions that are then vividly remembered, from many of life's memories combined with imagination**. Phew ! What happened to **'in and arising from one moment' alone?**

Just how reliable or unreliable, fulsome or fragmentary, is your/our/my memory? Some are blessed; I do not seem to be, struggling at times, feeling there is **more (embedded in memory, to enrich clarity of the verses)** ! I hope, Beginners, for your better memory.

This is haiku and psychology ! Where do these images come from? Our previously mentioned London haiku poet thought that we 'organised the 'Possibilities', through intellect discriminating above the senses': here and now images - stored in the memory and 'mind's eye. Another poet speaks about our many personal experiences; including pondering the Cosmos; books read; stories heard; even great cinema/television dialogue; and gained from our researches.

We have enjoyed and learned from the observations, brevity and simplicity of the ancient Japanese 'four recognised greats':

Matsuo Basho (d. 1694), Yosa Buson (d. 1783), Kobayashi Issa (d. 1827), and Masaoka Shiki (d.1902).

Forgive me, I have not tried to honour them, respectfully, in this book; for Beginners researching have a huge 'library' of poet-authors' writings and anthologies available on them and their works, far superior to anything I might attempt. Their works and words live on: 'The eternal intersects their everyday' said my London/ travelled/speaking Japanese poet.

I just bow, this intellect, his and mine, and concede its marvels — both at the bounteous riches offered all the senses by Nature, and our sufficiency in our sensitive human qualities in appreciating and composing Nature's delightful haiku and often naughty senryu.

Haiku is mainly serious and austere. We human also are serious, in our searches BUT beyond our seemingly lack of Divine knowledge, we also DO 'laugh at our smaller selves WHEN we Sincerely 'remember our true selves'. I hope, readers/Beginners, that you have enjoyed, even learned? Thus far. My compliments to all.

> Foot up, toe wriggles,
> Body's living miracle
> see, wave with yourSelf

Nature and haiku
honour life and our Selves:
just go with the flow

*I do hope you've enjoyed
your journey*

Goodbye for now

*Brian William Jarvis,
Reading UK*

Spring-Summer 2023

Give back to the Lord
gifts in body, mind, spirit:
work not to hold back

Printed in Great Britain
by Amazon

36593105R00086